THE HOW AND WHY WONDER BOOK OF
BIRDS

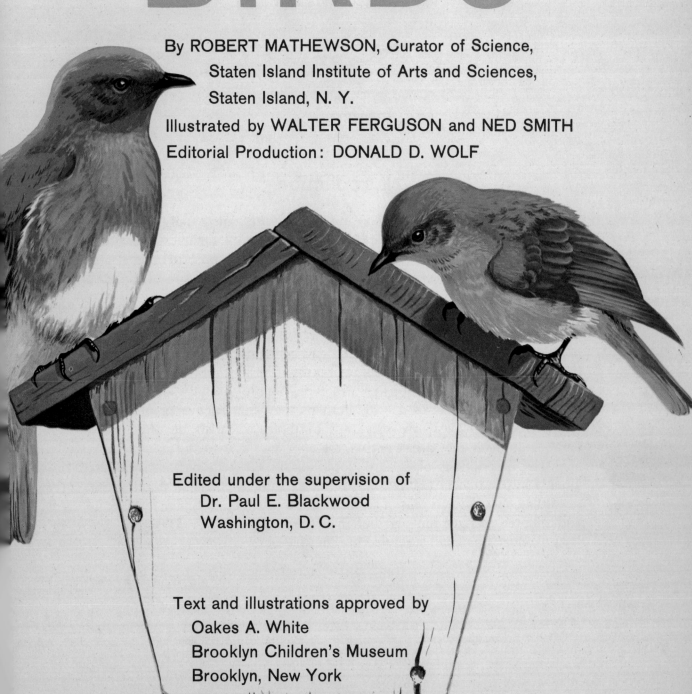

By ROBERT MATHEWSON, Curator of Science,
Staten Island Institute of Arts and Sciences,
Staten Island, N. Y.

Illustrated by WALTER FERGUSON and NED SMITH

Editorial Production: DONALD D. WOLF

Edited under the supervision of
Dr. Paul E. Blackwood
Washington, D. C.

Text and illustrations approved by
Oakes A. White
Brooklyn Children's Museum
Brooklyn, New York

GROSSET & DUNLAP • **Publishers** • **NEW YORK**

White-throated Sparrow

Introduction

"What bird is that?" is a question children ask almost daily. Grownups often wonder about birds, too, even if they don't ask their questions aloud. This colorful book not only tells about the more common birds, but it also introduces us to some uncommon and unusual ones. Have you ever seen a road runner? a condor? a cassowary? This *How and Why Wonder Book* tells about these and many more.

Much is known about birds, but there is still more to be learned. By observing and studying birds, children can contribute further knowledge to the science of *ornithology* (the study of birds). Perhaps they can add a more accurate description. Perhaps they can explain more carefully some habit or behavior characteristic of a bird. Perhaps they can discover a previously unobserved fact. These are the kinds of things scientists do. And when children do them, they are scientists, too.

The descriptions of several dozen birds will help persons who are already bird watchers (*birders*) and will encourage others to develop this rewarding hobby. Few areas of science offer a better opportunity for parents and children to have fun together than the study of birds. This *How and Why Wonder Book* will surely add to that pleasure.

Paul E. Blackwood

Dr. Blackwood is a professional employee in the U. S. Office of Education. This book was edited by him in his private capacity and no official support or endorsement by the Office of Education is intended or should be inferred.

Library of Congress Catalog Card Number: 72-86058

ISBN: 0-448-05009-9 (Wonder Book Edition)
ISBN: 0-448-04007-7 (Deluxe Edition)

Contents

RHAMPHORHYNCHUS

PTERANODON

ORNITHOLESTES

The World of Birds

If there were no eggs, where would birds come from? If there were no birds, where would eggs come from? Which came first—the egg or the bird? These questions seem to have no answer. However, the solution is really quite simple.

It all started about 200 million years ago when the dinosaurs, which were reptiles, roamed the earth. At this time, some of the smaller dinosaurs made their homes among the rocks in high cliffs. This kind of habitat offered protection from the large meat-eating dino-saurs that were too heavy to climb across the loose rocks.

It was here that the *Pterodactyls* (ter-o-DACK-tils) were found. They were fly-ing reptiles and flight helped them to escape an enemy or to swoop down and catch food. Some of the *Pterodactyls* (which means "wing finger") grew to enormous size. *Ornithostoma* (or-nee-THOS-to-ma) was the largest of all flying crea-

Could some prehistoric dinosaurs fly?

ARCHAEOPTERYX

ARCHAEOPTERYX

HESPERORNIS

ICHTHYORNIS

tures. The present-day albatross, with its wingspread of approximately eleven feet, is small compared to *Ornithostoma* (which means "bird mouth"). *Ornithostoma* was born with a ten-foot wingspread and, as an adult, had a wing span of over twenty feet. Like most *Pterodactyls,* it had a large bony head which helped to counterbalance its three-foot-long beak. Its wings were of skin, somewhat similar to those of modern bats.

During this period, many small reptiles were developing a character which was eventually to separate them from the reptile group. They were slowly evolving feathers. *Archaeopteryx* (ar-kee-OP-ter-iks, meaning "ancient wing") was the most familiar of these early birdlike reptiles. It had large and perfectly formed feathers on its wings and tail and had also developed birdlike legs. Other kinds, such as *Odontotormae* (o-DON-toe-tor-may, meaning "toothed bird") and *Ichthyornis* (ik-thee-OR-nis, meaning "fish bird"), had even more birdlike characteristics and were about the size of present-day gulls.

All of the early reptiles had one trait in common—they laid eggs. The next time you hear the question, "Which came first—the bird or the egg?" you will know the answer:

The reptile came first.

Today we have many kinds of birds—
20,000 different species—and they come in all sizes, forms and colors. There are gaudily colored parrots and macaws in tropical America; large flightless cassowaries and emus in Australia; tiny

How many kinds of birds are there?

warblers and sparrows in temperate America; soaring gulls and vultures in the world over; and plump chickens and turkeys in the farmyard.

Can you imagine Thanksgiving dinner without turkey? Of course, we could eat chicken or roast ham and perhaps some people would rather have them. If there never had been turkeys we would not miss them. However, just suppose there were no woodpeckers or other insect-eating birds. We would all miss them, because it wouldn't be long before the whole world was overrun by many hundreds of thousands of troublesome insects, eating away at plants and trees.

What good are birds?

We could keep these pests under control by using chemicals. Indeed, many pests are being controlled by chemicals now. But these poisons have proved to be more dangerous to birds and plants than to pests.

Anyone who has heard the *rat-a-tat-tat* of the woodpecker has had the opportunity to see at first hand the great insect-eating value of birds. A strong

What do birds eat?

There are about 375 species of woodpeckers. Their sharp bills bore into the bark of trees for insects. Below are some insect pests eaten by birds.

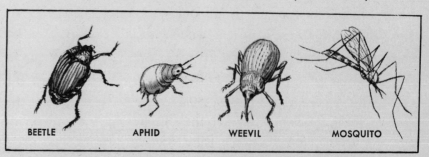

BEETLE   APHID   WEEVIL   MOSQUITO

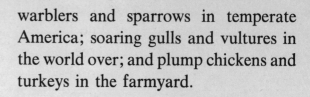

beak and neck muscles are the tools of the woodpecker. They enable the bird to cut its way through the tree bark to the insect feeding on the wood below. A special tongue, which is barbed, helps the woodpecker to stab, withdraw, and eat the insect. Most birds, at some time in their lives, feed upon insects.

House wrens, when raising a family, have been seen to carry more than sixty insects to their young in as many minutes. Suppose *you* were asked to catch sixty insects—do you think you could catch that many in an hour?

Birds also act as scavengers. Species such as gulls, vultures, crows, as well as hawks and owls, help to keep our woodlands and fields free of carrion (the flesh of dead animals).

Other important things about birds, particularly to those who spend some time watching them, are their bright, cheery colors and habits, and their beautiful songs.

Birding Is Fun

Watching birds, learning to identify the

Why should you watch birds?

different kinds by their shape, color and song, is a hobby which can bring many moments of real pleasure. It can change an ordinary walk through the park, the woodland or even the city street into an exciting adventure. The ways of these feathered fliers are soon learned and some become old "friends." Whether they hop, run or walk, and whether they fly in spurts or straight lines are some of the habits which aid in identifying each kind.

Even their songs will become familiar. The music of the wood thrush is pleasant to all. The song soon becomes associated with the bird and is often used in helping to identify it. In the park, the robins and sparrows will be known; in the woodland, the thrush and towhee; in the field, the meadowlark and pheasant; and at the beach, the gull and pelican. These and many

7

FLICKER

TUFTED TITMOUSE

HOODED WARBLER

BLUEJAY

of the other birds can make bird watching very interesting.

A good pair of binoculars is the most expensive single piece of equipment needed, but it is not absolutely necessary. Your eyes and ears are really all that are needed. However, the thrill of being able to bring a distant songster into clear view or to check carefully a treetop resident, makes binoculars desirable.

What tools are needed for birding?

A "bird guide" book will help in checking finds. One that fits into the pocket and can be taken into the field is most convenient. Cover it with a piece

THE MAIN FEATHER TRACTS OF THE WING

SECONDARIES

COVERTS

PRIMARIES

FEATHERS OF MANY COLORS AND FORMS

BILLS FOR:

CRUSHING

TEARING

PROBING

SKIMMING

LEGS AND FEET FOR:

PERCHING

RUNNING

SWIMMING

of waterproof plastic to protect it from soiling and wear.

Bird cards (available from Audubon societies) or a pocket notebook will enable you to make a record of your observations. Most bird watchers, or birders, as they are called, compile a "life list," which is a record of the many different species seen during their years of bird watching. This kind of record will prove more and more interesting as it grows.

How should you look for birds? Birds are with us winter, spring, summer and fall, and every nook and corner of our earth has its bird population. The only requirement for seeing them is to do it quietly. A few moments spent standing, sitting or slowly walking in a city park, an open field or woodland grove will reveal many more birds than will hours of strenuous hiking. Birds have keen eyesight and hearing and are very timid

9

animals. They will avoid a noisy observer.

A good bird watcher studies birds in his area. Repeated trips along the same paths and trails disclose where and upon what they feed, where they bathe and drink, where they nest and even in what trees they choose to sing. This kind of observing will be rewarded by the discovery of many facts about their habits. Not all of the breeding, nesting and feeding habits of birds are known, and good observers can add much to our scientific knowledge.

Birds in Flight

The careful birder soon learns to identify birds by their flight. The wavy course of the flicker, the upswept darting of the goldfinch and the soaring of the marsh hawk are as different as the sizes and shapes of these birds.

How do birds' feathers work?

Feathers, which evolved from the body scales of reptile ancestors, are an important part of the birds' flying equipment. They are strong and light in weight. Along the sides of the feathers are barbs which, if separated, look like fringe, or the branched ends which stick out from a piece of cloth. Each barb ends in a hook, which makes it possible for the barbs to hook on to one another. In this way a strong but very light flying wing is formed.

Internally, birds have air sacs and hollow bones which weigh less than solid flesh and bone. With less weight birds fly better. Even their streamlined form is ideally shaped for flight.

Flight is not confined to birds alone. Insects; fish (flying fish); frogs (Borneo flying frogs); snakes (Malayan flying snake); mammals (bats, phalangers, squirrels) have also taken to the air. However, there is no doubt that birds are the best fliers.

Are birds the best fliers?

A soaring eagle is a beautiful sight. It appears to be suspended from an invisible wire hooked in the clouds above. However, close watching through binoculars will show that even though the bird appears to be lazily gliding, it

How do birds fly?

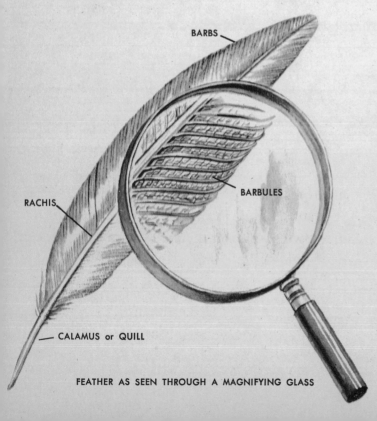

BARBS

RACHIS

BARBULES

CALAMUS or QUILL

FEATHER AS SEEN THROUGH A MAGNIFYING GLASS

The bird on the wing: A step-by-step picture sequence of a white stork taking off and rising on warm air.

is actually very active. Its outer wing feathers (primaries) and tail feathers are in constant motion, catching updrafts of warm air, and steering the bird through these ever-moving air currents. By showing these large upward moving columns of warm air as (A), and their neighboring downdrafts of cooler air as (B), we can understand more easily how eagles, vultures, hawks, gulls and other soaring birds stay aloft.

Like other objects which are heavier than air, birds in flight are constantly falling. When a bird is in an updraft of warm air (A) it is carried up more quickly than it falls. At this time, it can gain altitude. The bird now tries to keep itself in this column of air by steering with its wing and tail feathers.

When the bird moves into the column of downward moving air (B) it falls rapidly. However, it now uses its wings to help it glide, as quickly as possible, into another column of upward moving warm air (A). The speed that the bird attained while gliding downward in the "cool column" enables it to sweep upward more quickly when it enters the "warm column."

There are four types of bird flight: *flapping, dynamic soaring, static soaring* and *gliding*. We have already mentioned two—static soaring, as the bird steers and floats on the updraft, and gliding, as it moves through the downdraft.

How many kinds of flight are there?

Dynamic soaring is used by birds

11

The bluebird (left) and the robin (right) are songbirds.

The cardinal bird's full name is the cardinal grosbeak. It has a cone-like bill.

The common grackle (left), as its name indicates, makes a rough, harsh sound. The red-winged blackbird mixes whistling notes, squeaks and throaty calls.

like the albatross and pelican. By heading into the wind, they use the force of the moving air to carry them up. After they have attained sufficient height or when the wind slackens, they glide quickly downward, gaining the forward speed necessary to reach new winds. These birds live near or over the ocean where air is constantly blowing across the open water.

Flapping is the most complicated type of flight. All birds fly in this manner at some time, especially during take-off. At this time, the hand part of the wing (the end which has primary feathers) is used to propel air backward, and in this way the bird gets a forward push. While the wings appear to be going straight up and down they are really going in a somewhat circular fashion. When the wing is lifted and brought forward, the primary feathers

RED-WINGED BLACKBIRD

COMMON GRACKLE

separate and allow air to pass between them. On the downstroke the feathers close tightly together, forming a flat wing surface which forces the air backward. The part of the wing nearest the body (the arm) does not move as much as the outer part (the hand), and is used by the bird as a lifting surface in a way similar to the wing of an airplane.

Bluejays sometimes eat the eggs of smaller birds.

All birds shed their feathers, (a process called *molting*), and grow a new set at least once a year. Some birds go through this process twice. During the molting period, some species are awkward and unable to defend themselves. These seek hiding places and live quietly until their "suit" is completed. If molting did not take place, the feathers would soon look very seedy and the bird would be unable to fly.

Why do birds molt?

The Baltimore oriole is sometimes called the hangnest from a habit of hanging its nest from the tip of a branch.

The actual size of the chipping sparrow is shown in the illustration. Chippies, as they are called, sing faster as the weather gets warmer. They eat seeds.

Birds of Town and Field

Robins

Perhaps no bird is better known than the robin. People in the United States, Canada, and even Alaska are familiar with this rather plump ten-inch bird with its gray back and rusty red breast. It is a member of the thrush family, which includes the beautiful bluebird and the sweet-singing wood thrush. Its clear flutelike song is heard every morning, rain or shine, sounding as if it were happy to be alive.

The true robin, a smaller bird of similar coloring living in Europe, was so loved by the early English settlers, that they gave its name to this American bird.

There is always something happening in the life of a robin and it is an interesting bird to watch. It hops across the lawn or field, stopping every few feet, cocks its head to one side, and closely examines the ground for the hapless grub or insect that may be there. After a heavy rain the robin can often be seen tugging at one end of a large night crawler—an earthworm—which is trying desperately to escape down its burrow with its other end.

Do robins announce spring? Many people make the mistake of saying that spring is here as soon as they see a robin. It is true that most robins go south to warmer weather when it gets cold, but some robins stay north throughout the winter, finding their food on elderberry, sumac, mulberry and other bushes.

How do robins build nests? Their nest is built by both parents in a small tree or bush and sometimes under the eaves of a roof. It is constructed of mud, twigs and straw. First, pellets of mud, gathered at the edge of a stream or pond, are brought to the site and pushed together to form an egg-shaped base. Twigs are glued to this base by more mud, and grass or straw is woven between the twigs. The inner part of the nest is lined with fine soft grass where as many as five blue-green eggs are laid sometime in May, June or July.

AMERICAN ROBIN

EUROPEAN ROBIN

A bright spring morning is the best time to hear the European robin (left) and the American robin (right).

FOX SPARROW

TREE SPARROW

SAVANNA SPARROW

Sparrows

The ninety-two different species of sparrows found in the United States are members of the world's largest family of birds, which includes more than 500 kinds.

The European house sparrow, sometimes called the English sparrow, is really not a sparrow at all, but a weaver bird that has lived close to man for many hundreds of years. They were brought from England to the eastern United States in 1850, with the hope that they would eat the many caterpillars which were then stripping the leaves from trees. Within a few years, these birds were so numerous that they spread clear across the country, becoming a serious pest and crowding out many of our native birds.

Are sparrows native birds?

Most of the native sparrows are colored in somewhat the same soft tones of brown, tan and black. The fat little fox sparrow has rusty-colored breast stripes and reddish cheek patches. The roly-poly chipping sparrow has a white throat and breast, brown wings and red topknot. Both birds have colors and patterns which make them attractive.

The swamp, song, white-throat, ipswich, seaside, lark and tree sparrows are all talented songsters. But no more sweet and sprightly tune is heard outdoors than that of the song sparrow. It starts with three short, strong calls and is followed by a variety of notes which always end so quickly that one feels the sparrow didn't have time to finish its song.

Can sparrows sing?

15

Most sparrows eat seeds, often feeding upon the food that man has grown for himself. However, a great part of their diet is made up of insects, particularly during the nesting season, when both parents carry insects to feed their young. Their love for seeds brings these birds close to our homes, and many different kinds visit the backyard, neighboring lot or field. Unlike the house sparrows, which build their nests close to human habitation, the true sparrows nest in the woodlands.

What do sparrows eat?

Ruby-throated Hummingbird

This interesting bird of the eastern United States is one of the smallest known. Its first cousin, the calliope hummingbird of California, reaches a size of three inches, whereas the ruby-throat grows to be four inches in length. They are the best fliers in birdland. They can fly straight up or down, forward or backward, and if necessary can hover in one spot for many minutes. Their short wings move so very fast that they appear as a blur.

The humming sound of their moving wings and the ruby-red feathers at the throat, which stand out in strong contrast to the pale whitish feathers of the breast and stomach, have earned them their name.

How did they get their name?

RUBY-THROATED HUMMINGBIRDS

Hummingbirds bind their nests with spider webs.

The greenish feathers along the back, sides, wings and head have a bluish-green iridescence, which is particularly brilliant at the sides of the head. This sheen glistens in the sunlight and, when the bird is resting, it looks like a sparkling jewel.

Small hummingbirds are often mistaken for large insects and sometimes a large bird will pursue them, perhaps thinking it is chasing a moth. However, hummingbirds are so quick in their flight that they soon outdistance the larger bird. This extraordinary skill in flying makes them unafraid, and they can occasionally be seen teasing larger birds by flying at them, perhaps hoping to have the fun of being chased.

These small birds are at home in the **How do they eat?** fields, brush and forest. They can also be found around homes, particularly if honeysuckle or trumpet vine is growing nearby. Their extremely long beaks—almost one fourth as long as the bird—are inserted into the bell-like flowers; and the tongue, which is a double-barreled tube, sucks up the sweet nectar found in a sac at the base of the flower. Hummingbirds also eat many small insects.

The small white eggs, only one half to three quarters of an inch **Where do they lay their eggs?** long, are very fragile and are laid in a tiny nest lined with soft spider web or planted down to protect them. The outside of the nest is covered with pieces of bark and lichen plants, and blends so well with the surroundings that the eggs are rarely seen.

Starlings

Starlings were brought to the United States from Europe in 1870. When first introduced, these birds showed a preference for living in the fields and woodlands and their food was mainly insects. However, they soon found an abundance of suitable food in fruit orchards and in the refuse and garbage found in parks and city streets. As they increased in numbers, they crowded out the house sparrow.

The large eight-inch starlings are quite handsome, especially the **Do their colors vary?** males. When they are in their breeding plumage, they have shiny greenish-black body

17

Starlings were first brought to the U.S. from Europe.

They are great mimics, and often you will hear the notes of a robin or song sparrow coming from a tree, only to discover that the owner of the voice is a starling that has borrowed the tune.

However, not everything about this bird is bad. It still is a handsome creature and the amount of good it does by eating insects outweighs the damage it does to fruit crops.

Warblers

When spring comes to the Temperate Zone it brings the warblers. They follow the warmth, as they come north, back to their summer homes. In great numbers they race across the branches of trees, shrubs and bushes peering here and there, visiting each leaf and bud in their constant search for insects.

feathers and a blue-black iridescent sheen on the head and throat feathers. The bill is a bright yellow. In winter, the younger birds have a dark bill and a pattern of light spots on the body feathers. Females are always drab brown to black with a slight iridescence on the shoulders and head.

Because of their great numbers they

Are starlings useful birds? have become a problem in many cities. They roost by the thousands on the window ledges and masonry of large buildings, and their droppings spoil the looks of these places. Being large and quarrelsome permits them to steal the nesting sites of other birds. They also steal the songs of other birds.

There are over one hundred different kinds of warblers in the United States, and they **How many kinds of warblers are there?** are all small, four to six inches long. Because of the great variety and brilliance of their coloring, they have been called "butterflies of the bird world." One of the most brilliant is the male eastern yellow warbler. Its yellow body with striped red breast is like a flash of sunlight as it darts in and out of the new green of spring growth.

The nests of warblers can be found from northern Canada **Where do they build their nests?** to the southern United States. They are built of twigs, grass and moss, and are sometimes tied together with pieces of spider or caterpillar web. The myrtle warbler, a small black and white striped bird with patches of yellow on the head, base of the tail, and sides of the body, builds its nest in small pine, spruce or hemlock trees in the evergreen forests. The yellow warbler seeks brush or briar patches, and the nests of the Cape May warbler are often built on the ground. Warblers are protected and encouraged to build their nests near fruit orchards. There they help the farmer by finding insects both for themselves and their young.

Bluejays

These large twelve-inch birds are the noisiest inhabitants of our woodlands. They can be found throughout the eastern United States, from the Mississippi River to the Atlantic Ocean. Like the robin, starling and sparrow they often take up residence in or near a town. However, they also frequent the deepest parts of the forest.

When in danger, and even sometimes when not, bluejays will scream their alarm cry. The call is not unlike a squeaky pulley and is given over and over, while the birds

How do they protect their nests?

BLACK-THROATED WARBLER

PARULA WARBLER

CANADA WARBLER

MAGNOLIA WARBLER

bounce up and down on their perches, flitting back and forth in great excitement. The noise and antics are usually all bluff, for if the danger gets too close, they quickly give ground and scramble for safety. However, during the nesting season, brooding birds have been seen to attack a marauding cat by flying at its head and pecking until the cat decided it would be happier elsewhere.

Both parents help in building the nest. It is made of twigs and grass and is anchored high off the ground in a tall tree. When built near human habitation the nest often contains string, paper, rags and other by-products of civilization. Two to five varicolored eggs are laid sometime in May or June. They take a little over two weeks to hatch.

Bluejays protect a nest by frightening off visitors.

The bluejay is handsome and immediately after molting, in late August to November, it is clothed in a brilliant coat of blue, gray, black and white. Its head crest of bright blue feathers, outlined in black, gives it a striking crown, and the bright new blue of the wing and tail feathers, with their accents of black and white, is most attractive. The colors of females are similar, except they are less bright.

When do bluejays molt?

Bluejays are often considered a menace because they raid the nests of other birds, killing and eating the young. Their usual diet consists of insects, fruits and nuts. They are great hoarders and will take away more food than they can eat. They hide this extra supply in the crevices of the bark or crotches of trees. Perhaps they seek out and eat this food later, for they do not migrate far and some bluejays stay in the north throughout the winter.

Do bluejays migrate?

Scientists who have made careful studies of these birds tell us that bluejays do much more good than harm.

RAVEN

COMMON CROW

Birds of Woodland and Forest

Crows

Some hunters claim that crows know the distance their bullets can reach, because these birds always stay just outside of gunshot.

Whether the crow can judge the effective range of a gun is seriously doubted. However, their reputation for shrewdness has been well earned. They are extremely wary birds, usually traveling in flocks. It is believed, and with good reason, that they post sentries high in the trees, at the edge of a feeding ground, or at the roost where they sleep. If danger approaches, these sentries sound the alarm in time for the others to fly away.

Ravens

The common raven of the old world, in northern United States and Canada, is twenty-six inches long and is the largest of the three all-black birds called crows. They live in the forests and on high cliffs along the coast. Ravens' nests are crude affairs constructed of strong sticks, lined with seaweed and grass, and built in the tops of tall pines or on inaccessible rocks. The birds are excellent parents and will defend the nest and young with their lives.

Common Crow

The well known common crow is found throughout the United States and Mexico. Like its larger cousins, it is a bird of the woodlands. However, very early in the morning, long before sun-up, large flocks will venture into town streets and backyards seeking food.

This bird measures twenty inches and, if seen alone, is hard to distinguish from the raven. But the raven's voice, larger size and wedge-shaped tail distinguish it from the crow. The call of the raven is a hoarse *cr-r-r-cruk* sound, while the call of the crow is a distinct *caw-caw-caw*.

Like ravens, crows build their nests high in the trees, but their nests are better constructed, being built of sticks and lined with strips of bark, vines, dry grass, leaves and moss. Outwardly they appear to be very rough, but the lining in snug and warm. The eggs and babies are well protected by the parents. They will often continue to feed their young even after the young have left the nest.

Fish Crows

The fish crow is the smallest of this group, although large specimens sometimes reach the size of the common crow. Here, again, the voice affords the only sure method of identifying it. The call consists of a coarse *car-car-car*. As their name suggests, fish crows are more often found near the coast or along river valleys where they feed upon fish, clams or crustaceans. They fly above the water in search of food and, unlike the common crow, will hover in flight when food is discovered. Nests and nesting sites are similar to those of the common crow.

Fish crows also prey upon the eggs of other birds. Similarly, crows raid the nests of other birds and eat their young, and the raven will steal young fowl from farmyards. In many areas they are considered pests and are hunted, but all three birds are mainly scavengers and do more good for man than harm.

Chirps, whistles, and songs are the language of the birds.

What do bird calls mean?

Each species has its own set of sounds, different from those of all other species. People who have observed birds as they call and sing have discovered that these sounds have a very precise meaning to other birds. Birds utter their first sounds while they are still in the nest. The gaping beaks and pitiful cries tell the mother that her babies want food. Adult birds may utter a *feeding call* to alert other birds that food is nearby. The signal invites the entire flock to join the meal. The herring gull and other species finish their own meal before making their feeding calls.

Migrating birds make *contact calls* that help keep the flock together. The contact call is simply an announcement that a bird is looking for others of the same species, a kind of recognition signal which says, "I'm over here. Where are you?" Nearby birds of the same species may take up the call, and the entire flock may join in a chorus of calls. Contact calls also help birds of the same species to find each other at night or when they are hidden amid thick vegetation.

Assembly calls rally the flock together. *Flight calls* arouse the flock to follow the caller in migratory flight. *Alarm calls* warn other members of the flock that danger lurks nearby. One type of alarm call indicates that the enemy is a flying predator, such as a hawk or falcon. The place from which this call comes is difficult to locate, so that the caller is also protected from the hawk. If the predator is on the ground, the caller chirps a different danger call which helps the other birds locate the enemy.

Each species may have from one to two dozen different sounds. Sometimes the calls of different species are very similar. Every bird seems to be born with the ability to recognize the sound of others in its species. But some sounds may be recognized by more than one species, especially alarm calls. Other calls are recognized only by a particular flock or group of birds. These calls are like a local "dialect" within the language of the species.

Cries of chicks in nest stimulate bird parents to bring food.

Mynah birds and parrots are the best mimics. They can learn to utter complete sentences, although words have no meaning for them.

A bird song is a train of musical sounds

Why do birds sing?

different from a chirp or whistle. The singer is usually the male of the species, who performs during the breeding season. The song has a dual purpose: (1) to keep other males away from the singer's territory and (2) to attract a female of the same species. The male stakes his claim to a feeding and nesting area by singing his song at various "song posts" in his territory. Other males are warned away by the sound and females are attracted to it. Once a female has been lured into the male's territory, his song becomes softer and sweeter. The courtship song stimulates the birds to nest, without attracting enemies.

Some tropical birds sing duets. The male and female have different songs, which they sing either simultaneously or in response to each other. Each pair of birds has its own particular pair of songs, which help the mated birds find each other in thick tropical jungles.

Some birds are born with knowledge of their songs already fixed in their brain. Other species are born knowing only a few notes; and the remaining flourishes of the song are learned by imitating adult birds of the species.

There are birds who mimic the songs of other species. Starlings and mockingbirds can mimic parts of the songs of many different species. The best mimics of all, parrots and mynah birds, can mimic human speech. These "talking birds" may utter a hundred different words and repeat entire sentences. One parrot learned to say "Don't forget to shut the door" whenever anyone left the room. But the words have no meaning to the bird. They were probably learned by the parrot in order to attract its keeper. Often, such "talking" birds do most of their chattering when they are alone. Perhaps their speech is a cry for social contact with the species they are mimicking — namely, human beings.

BARN OWL

PYGMY O

SCREECH OWL

24

GREET HORNED OWL

SNOWY OWL

Owls

Owls are naturally birds of the forests,
deserts and jungles.
However, there are
those which have
taken up life in
barns, church steeples and even in trees
in the town park. They occur in many
parts of the world. There are the giant
Pell's fishing owls of the African forest,
with their large talons which clasp fish
caught in the running streams, and
eight-inch saw-whet owls, and screech
owls that call from their nests in the
city parks in the United States.

Where do owls live in the daytime?

They are active at night, and their
hoots, shrieks and
calls can be heard
throughout the sea-
sons. We can imitate these calls to learn
their whereabouts, and then illuminate
the birds by using a strong flashlight.
Absolute quiet and slow, careful move-
ments are necessary for success in this
kind of birding. Owls' night sight is
keen, and they can hear exceptionally
well. A twig broken underfoot is
enough to warn them.

How can owls be seen?

With their sharp eyes and wings that
make no sound in flight,
they have become expert
at catching rodents, rab-
bits and other small
mammals that make up their food. The
false belief that owls cannot see in the
daytime probably comes from their inability to see unless the object is directly
ahead of their eyes. If they wish to look

Can owls see in the daytime?

25

to one side, they have to turn their heads in that direction, and they can actually rotate their heads so that they can see directly over their backs. But owls can see, of course, in the daytime.

Snowy Owl

This owl of the Arctic, Canada and the northern part of the United States, in its predominantly white plumage, is well camouflaged in snow. It is a large bird, twenty-seven inches tall with a wingspread of over five feet. Occasionally it may be driven south by severe winter storms. These birds make their nests high in the mountains above the tree line, usually in open, barren country. The nest is nothing more than a depression in the ground.

Great Horned Owl

The great horned owl is slightly smaller than the snowy owl and lives in the deep forests of Canada and the United States. The abundance of rodents around human habitations often lures them to the woodlands near towns. They are easily recognized by the horn-like tufts of feathers growing from either side at the front of the head. They rarely build nests, but use those abandoned by hawks and crows.

Birds of the Desert

Burrowing Owl

These small owls, residents of the deserts of the Southwest, are ten inches tall. They do not build nests, but use the abandoned burrows of the prairie dog (a small ground rodent). Rattlesnakes, gophers and owls make use of these burrows, but not all at the same

The burrowing owl prefers the nest of some ground mammal rather than any nest of its own construction.

The powerfully-legged roadrunner seldom flies, but runs with great speed. It is the rattlesnake's chief enemy.

time. Burrowing owls feed on grasshoppers and other insects, and small rodents. Unlike most other owls they do their hunting in the daytime.

Roadrunner

This slender bird of the southwestern United States and Mexico, also known as the chaparral cock or snake killer, is a member of the cuckoo family. It reaches a length of almost two feet, half of which is made up of a coppery green-colored tail. The back and head plumage is bronze-colored, and on each side of the head there is a short bright red stripe. Roadrunners rarely fly; however, their swiftness of foot is remarkable.

How do they catch their food? Reptiles such as snakes and lizards make up the main portion of their diet. When catching and killing a poisonous rattlesnake,

they will approach to within the snake's striking distance, with wings partially spread, head bobbing up and down, and steps gingerly carrying them from side to side. These antics are probably performed to tease the snake into striking and also to confuse it.

When the snake strikes, the bird very quickly jumps into the air out of harm's way. This performance is repeated many times. Finally the snake tires and it is then that the bird strikes out with its long sharp beak, delivering blows that soon maim and kill the reptile. After very carefully examining the snake to make sure it is dead, the roadrunner takes it by the head and swallows it whole.

The nest of this bird is a flimsy affair built of twigs, sometimes on the ground, but usually up in a small bush. A brood of six to eight are raised each year and are fed mostly insects and occasionally, a small lizard.

27

SPARROW HAWK

DUCK HAWK

ROUGH-LEGGED HAWK

Birds of the Sky

Hawks

More than 500 different forms of hawks inhabit many areas throughout the world. This large group includes the vultures, buzzards, eagles, falcons, hawks and kites. They are mainly birds of prey, catching and killing their food by striking it from the air and upon the ground. The exceptions to this are the buzzards and vultures, which usually find and eat carrion.

Falconry, the sport of hunting with trained hawks, eagles or falcons, has been practiced by men since ancient times. It started in China about 4,000 years ago and has been enjoyed in many countries since then.

Birds of this group perform a valuable service for man by feeding upon great numbers of rodents and other destructive small mammals. Some species, such as Cooper's hawk and the sharp-shinned hawk, do feed upon birds, and

SWALLOW-TAILED HAWK

CARACARA HAWK

COOPER'S HAWK

sometimes upon small fowl in unprotected farmyards.

Sparrow Hawk

Hawks vary greatly in size. The sparrow hawk is a small bird, about eight to ten inches, which occurs throughout the greater part of North America to as far south as Costa Rica.

Most of the hawks, both male and female, are somber in color. However, the buff-colored spotted breast, brown back and tail, soft blue-

Do they eat insects?

gray wings, and white and black cheeks with the topping of red on the head, make the male sparrow hawk a most attractive bird.

Unlike the larger hawks, these birds seek smaller prey, and when grasshoppers are available they feed almost wholly on these insects. They can and do catch mice and an occasional bird. They are firm protectors of their nests, which may be located almost anywhere —in a depression in the ground, the abandoned nest of another bird, a nook in an old building or even a cavity in a rotting tree stump.

29

BALD EAGLE

Duck Hawk

This bird was used in falconry by the knights and nobility of England in days gone by. The American duck hawk, found throughout most of North and South America, and the European bird are so similar that it is difficult to tell the differences between them.

It is most exciting to watch this master of flight while it is hunting. It can overtake and capture any bird, except possibly the swift and the hummingbird. The hunting flight starts high in the sky and after great speed is attained, the duck hawk half-folds its wings and moves so fast that one can hear the air as it rushes through the bird's feathers. At all times its flight is under control, for if the prey swerves, the duck hawk quickly alters course.

How do they catch their prey?

The force of the impact of being seized or struck by the powerful talons of the hawk renders the prey helpless. No other bird, not even the large eagles, will attempt to pilfer the duck hawk's nest. Little more than a few twigs and some small bits of moss, placed in the center as a lining, is used by the duck hawk in making a nest. Often the eggs will be laid on bare rock. The nest site is usually high up on the side of an inaccessible cliff.

Bald Eagle

Since ancient times the eagle has been regarded as a symbol of courage and power. Its keenness of vision, fierce appearance and majestic

Why is the bald eagle the U.S. National Emblem?

bearing made the Second Continental Congress, in 1782, vote this bird the National Emblem of the United States.

Eagles float on the air high above the ground, at times so far up that they appear as a mere speck against the blue. They have often been accused of swooping down and carrying off small children. These stories are untrue. Even though they are large birds, measuring as much as three feet long with a wingspread of seven feet, they could not lift the weight of a small child off the ground.

Can they carry off children?

Their food, mainly fish, is found dead on the beach, and sometimes stolen from smaller birds. If pressed by hunger they will hunt for themselves and there are many accounts of their chasing and capturing ducks and geese. Their nests are built of strong sticks on craggy cliff sides, high above the ground.

Condor

The California condor, found in the mountains of Lower California, and the South American condor are the largest birds that fly. They are approximately four and one half feet long and have a wingspread of eleven feet. The South American condor is found in the Andes Mountains and probably flies higher than any other bird, having been observed at altitudes of over 20,000 feet. It is a grotesque bird with black plumage and a bare head covered with wrinkled red skin, and at the top of the head it has a bright red comb.

How high do condors fly?

Like other vultures, both of these

SOUTH AMERICAN CONDOR

birds feed upon carrion; however, they will also attack and kill small mammals.

The Andean condor does not build a nest, but lays its eggs in a depression in a rock high in the mountains. The California bird is almost extinct.

Water Birds

Ducks

Ducks can be found the world over. They are usually seen in flocks on fresh-water ponds, lakes and swamps, and salt-water oceans, bays and inlets. The fondness for water is common to all of them, and they are able to swim rapidly because of a webbing of skin between their toes. They have oil glands on the body which provide a waterproof covering for their feathers. Those ducks that dive for their food are thus able to surface with dry wings, ready for flight on a moment's notice.

Geese are merely larger ducks, with male and female similar **Are geese and ducks related?** in color and pattern. The males of the smaller ducks are usually "clothed" in brighter colors.

Wood Duck

One of the most beautiful birds known is the eighteen-inch wood duck of the United States and Mexico. It is gaudily colored and unfortunately, the great beauty of these birds is a danger to them, because hunters seek them out as a prize. As many as twenty-four eggs are laid by the female in a nest in a hollow tree high off the ground.

Mallard Duck

Unlike the wood duck, the mallard builds its nest on the ground near a deep swamp, hidden by a dense growth of rushes and cattail plants. The nest is warmly lined with down feathers from the mother's breast.

These birds are of great economic importance. They are an excellent control for mosquitoes, which they catch in the larval stage (water form) of the insect's life cycle. Many farmers encourage the mallards' presence on the farm pond for this reason. They not only feed upon myriads of land insects, but they themselves are used by man as food. It is this duck, more than any other, that has been used for breeding purposes to produce many of the domesticated ducks used the world over.

COMMON TERN

MOOR HEN

SPOONBILL

WHITE STORK

LITTLE GREBE

HERON

STILTS

BLACK TERN

MARBLED DUCK

KENTISH PLOVERS

RUDDY SHELDUCK

FERRUGINOUS DUCK

Canada Goose

This goose has a body over three feet in length and a wingspread of almost six feet.

When the long V-formations of these geese fly overhead, spring or winter is not far away. This sight is exciting to behold and most people watch until the birds disappear over the horizon. Even though they are high in the sky, their honking calls can be heard quite clearly. These large birds usually build on the ground, constructing their nests of twigs, grasses and leaves, with the inner part lined with down. They choose a single mate for life, and at nesting time, if any animal approaches—even man— they will attack violently. The Canada geese make their homes on the North American Continent.

Where do they nest?

Birds of Beach and Ocean

Many different kinds of birds find their food and homes near the beach. These include the skimmer, a bird which glides along a few inches above the ocean, using its lower bill to skim food from just below the surface of the water.

What food do these birds eat?

Another is the sandpiper which races back and forth across the sand, catching sand fleas and other small crustaceans as they are exposed by the wash of the waves.

Most common of the beach birds are those we call sea gulls. There are many species of gulls and not all kinds are found near salt water. Some forms are found near inland waterways and lakes many hundreds of miles from the ocean. These birds are important to man because they feed upon refuse and carrion and thereby keep the beaches clean.

SANDPIPERS

SKIMMER

LESSER BLACK-BACKED GULL

COMMON GULL

LITTLE GULL

BLACK-HEADED GULL

HERRING GULL

MEDITERRANEAN GULL

These are some of the gulls that fly over the water.

Gulls also feed upon many insects. The great grasshopper plagues that visited the farms of the Mormon settlers in Utah were brought under control by gulls. A large statue of the gull, in commemoration of this deed, stands in Salt Lake City, Utah.

Herring Gull

Herring gulls are, by far, the most common. They occur by the thousands along the coast, particularly near towns and cities. They range throughout the greater part of the Northern Hemisphere, and in the Eastern Hemisphere they can be found in Iceland and Siberia and as far south as the Mediterranean and Caspian Seas. Although they appear small while on the wing, they are rather large, measuring twenty-six inches in length, with a wingspread just under five feet.

One of the gull's most interesting habits is to take a clam—which has proven too hard to break—into the air, and drop it upon a stone in order to expose the meaty food inside. In fishing villages where the "catch" is cleaned on the beach, these gulls make short work of the entrails, leaving the beach spotlessly clean.

Their nests, which are composed of eel grass, marsh grasses, weeds, sticks, feathers and shells are constructed along the coast of New England and Canada and on some coastal islands.

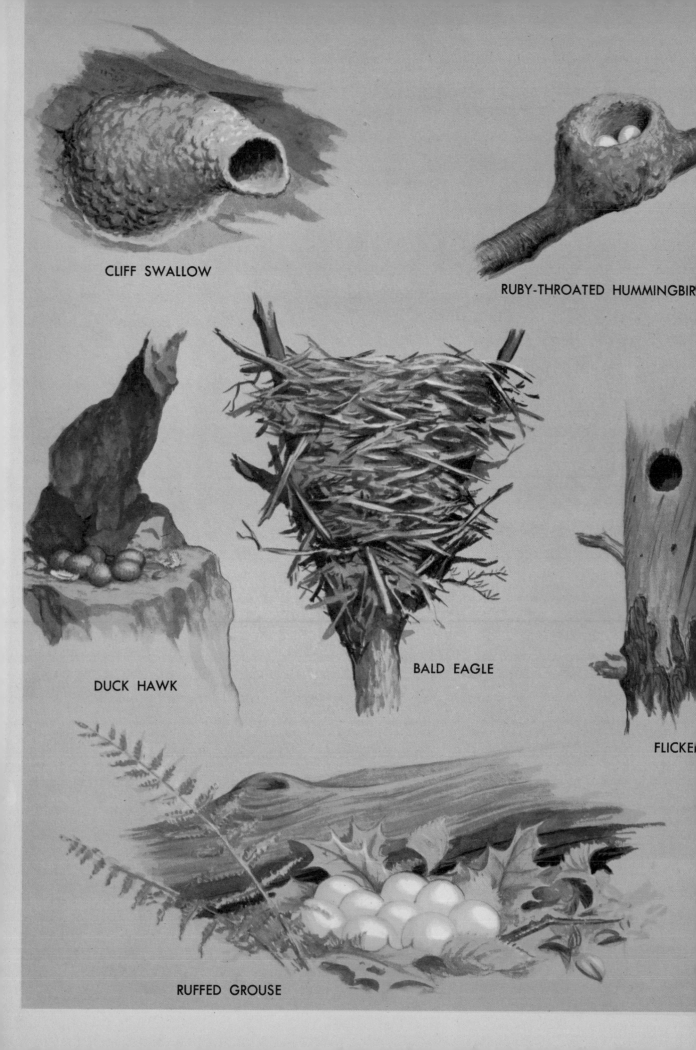

CLIFF SWALLOW

RUBY-THROATED HUMMINGBIR

DUCK HAWK

BALD EAGLE

FLICKE

RUFFED GROUSE

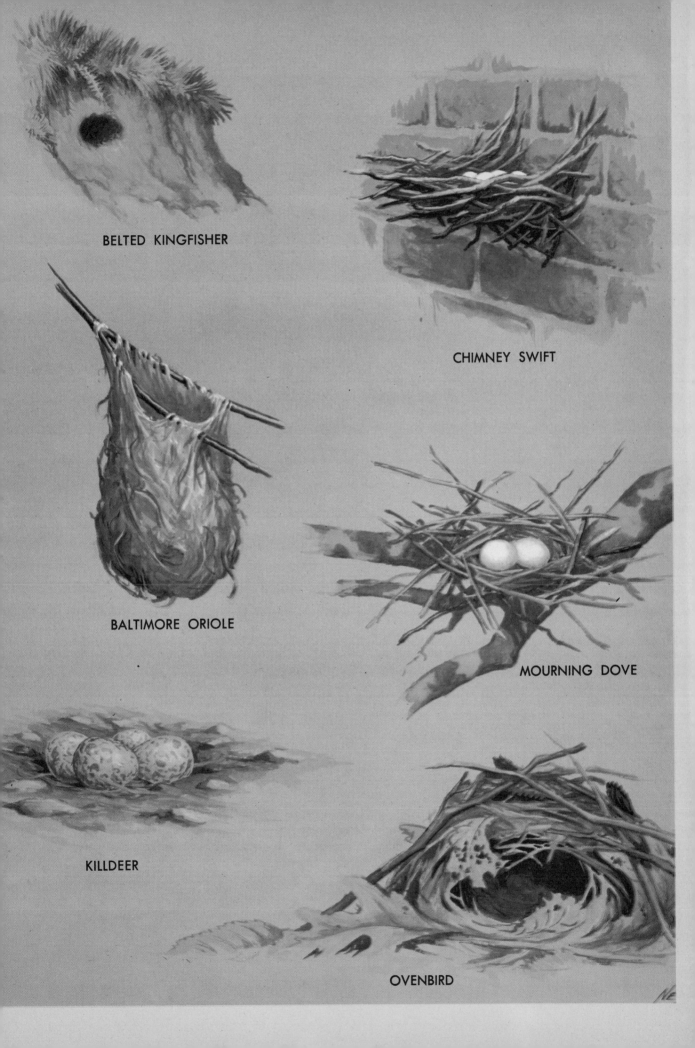

BELTED KINGFISHER

CHIMNEY SWIFT

BALTIMORE ORIOLE

MOURNING DOVE

KILLDEER

OVENBIRD

Pelicans

The brown pelican is found along the coastal waters of southern California, Florida, the Gulf, and the Atlantic coasts of Central and South America. Its lower mandible (beak) has a large fold of skin that serves as a net for catching fish. When a hungry pelican, soaring above the water, spies a fish, it folds its wings and dives into the water in pursuit. When it surfaces it will push the two or three gallons of water out of the distended pouch and swallow the captured fish whole.

A brown pelican feeds its young from the pouch.

These birds are comical, often gathering in groups and acting as if they were holding an important conference. They build their simple gravel and rubbish nests on small islands. Their one or two young receive food by placing their heads into the mother's gullet for recently captured fish, which she has partially digested.

The white pelican, found in the Western and Eastern Hemispheres, does not dive for food. It scoops up fish as it glides in the water. Often, groups of these pelicans move in line-formation to drive a school of fish into shallow water where they are caught.

White pelicans in flight. These aquatic birds move in flocks and they are related to gannets and cormorants.

The albatross brings good weather was an old tale.

Albatross

These graceful white birds are often seen from ocean liners that ply the waters of the southern Pacific. They are the largest of the ocean birds, with a wingspread that sometimes exceeds

The relative size of the albatross can be seen here.

eleven feet. However, in weight and body size, they are not as large as the mountain-dwelling condor. Their ability to soar on the constant winds over the ocean is exceeded by no other bird. Without a single wing beat they can fly for miles, sometimes gliding so close to the water that they momentarily disappear between the crests of the waves.

The antics of an albatross in becoming airborne are complicated. It runs rapidly across the surface of the water for many yards before gaining sufficient speed so that its long, thin, outspread wings can lift it into the air.

They breed on secluded oceanic islands in nests that are nothing more than cleared pieces of ground.

RED-CROWNED PARROT

KEEL-BILLED TOUCAN

BLUE-CROWNED CHLOROPHONIA

RED-LEGGED HONEY CREEPERS

Jungle Birds

Some of the most unusual birds in the world are found in the jungles. The variety of pattern, color and habits is so great that many books have been written about them. Few of us may ever have the opportunity to visit the jungles of Australia to observe the colorful lyre bird with its gracefully curved tail feathers—or to the South American rain forests to see the gaudily colored red, black and white toucan, with its large bright orange beak tipped with ivory black. However, we all can go to the local library, zoo or museum, and there see and read about the wonders of the bird world native to the distant jungles.

GREAT CURASSOW

QUETZAL

TURQUOISE-BROWED MOTMOT

GREEN JAY

BOAT-BILLED HERON

CRIMSON-COLORED TANAGER

SUN BITTERN

The hornbills are a family of birds having large bills.

Hornbill

This bird of the jungles of northern Africa, India and the East Indies derives its name from an immense bill and helmet, which give it a top-heavy, grotesque appearance.

Actually the bill, which is made of a hard spongy tissue, is quite light in weight. Even though it looks awkward and clumsy, the birds are quite adept at using it to catch insects and small rodents. They can also use it very delicately, for when catching grapes tossed by a zookeeper from ten feet away, they catch them without even breaking through the grape's skin.

Hornbills are known for their unique nesting habits. The female enters a hollow tree where she prepares her nest, usually laying but a single egg. The male bird seals off the opening with mud and saliva, leaving **How do they build a nest?** a small hole through which to give her the food he has partially digested. The female is not sealed in to keep her at home, but rather to protect her from marauders.

Cassowaries

The cassowary is one of the flightless birds that inhabit the forests of Australia and New Guinea.

Like the ostrich of Africa, the rhea of South America and the emu of southeastern Australia, the cassowary makes up for its inability to fly by being able to run extremely fast. It has large, strong legs, with three-toed feet, each of which has a sharp nail on the middle toe. Blows given with the foot can be dangerous.

The cassowary is smaller than the emu and the ostrich.

The impressive appearance of this five-foot-high bird is heightened by the violet color of the bare, heavily wrinkled skin of the neck and head. The hornlike projection on the top of the head is

How do they move through a jungle?

believed to protect the bird, by brushing aside the undergrowth as the cassowary bounds and leaps through the jungle at high speed.

These birds travel in pairs. The female uses the soft moss on the jungle floor as a nest for her five-inch eggs.

Birds of the Antarctic

Penguins

Even the land of ice and constant cold has its bird population. Penguins, the small flightless birds that stand upright and look like attentive waiters at a swank country club, are a prize exhibit at most zoos.

Do penguins build a nest?

The nesting habits of the king penguin, a species that lives in desolate, cold regions, are interesting. They keep their eggs from freezing by carrying them between the belly and feet. The incubation period lasts seven weeks, during which time the eggs are transferred from the male to the female.

Penguins are good swimmers, and the fish they catch are the main part of their diet. Not all of the sixteen different kinds live in the Antarctic. One species actually lives at the equator, on the Galapagos Islands.

The penguins are flightless birds living in the Southern Hemisphere. This is a colony of black-footed penguins.

The Mystery of Migration

Every spring and fall millions of birds all over the world take
What birds migrate? to the air. Large flocks of birds can be seen flying steadily in one direction, headed for some distant land. In North America, migrating birds generally head south in the fall and north in the spring. Golden plovers leave their breeding grounds in arctic Alaska and fly eight thousand miles to the plains of Argentina, crossing two thousand miles of open ocean. Some golden plovers fly thousands of miles across the trackless Pacific Ocean to the islands of Hawaii.

Bobolinks leave the clover fields of the Midwest for a long journey to the southernmost parts of South America. Tiny hummingbirds fly hundreds of miles across the Gulf of Mexico. Squadrons of Canada geese fly in precise V-formation as they head south, honking mournfully. Chimney swifts fly from Nova Scotia to Brazil. From Canada and the northern United States robins, hawks, and bluejays move south. Swallows leave southern California for South America. The white storks of northern Europe travel long distances to Africa and back each year.

The arctic tern holds the long-distance championship among migratory birds. During summer these birds breed in the northern portions of Canada, Europe, and Asia. In the fall, as winter approaches, they take off on an 11,000-mile journey to the southern tips of Africa and South America. In the spring they make a return trip to their nesting grounds, so that they fly about 22,000 miles each year.

Some birds migrate only short distances. They fly from the cold interior regions to the warmer ocean shores. And not all migrations are north and south. Some birds merely leave their mountain homes for the more protected valleys as winter approaches.

No one knows why birds get the urge to migrate. One obvious reason may be
Why do birds migrate? the loss of their food supply during winter. But this reason is unsatisfactory because the birds leave long before the first snows cover their food supply. Their brain cannot reason sufficiently to predict changes in the weather. So the migrating behavior seems to be instinctive (inborn), not learned. Young arctic terns born at their Arctic breeding grounds will take off with the flock for distant lands they have never seen.

According to some scientists, migratory birds should be able to withstand the winter. Their feathery coats are good insulation against cold. Being warm-blooded animals, they can adapt to winter conditions. It has been noted that some members of the same species, such as bluejays and hawks, remain in the north while others fly south for the winter.

Migratory birds seem to be born with certain biological processes that urge them to migrate. Scientists suspect that the changing length of the day is the

The arctic tern has the longest migration, flying from the Arctic to the Antarctic and back every year — a combined distance of about 22,000 miles.

BREEDING RANGE
FLYWAYS
WINTER HOME

GREENLAND
Arctic Circle
EUROPE
NORTH AMERICA
AFRICA
Equator
Pacific Ocean
SOUTH AMERICA
Atlantic Ocean
Antarctic Circle

fat. This stored fat is the fuel that provides the energy for a long flight. The same experiment revealed that the birds became more excited as the artificial night was lengthened. It's no coincidence that most flocks begin their migratory flights during the night.

Whatever its cause, the urge to migrate is strong and exists even in newborn birds who have never traveled. At one time it was believed that the older birds taught the younger ones the migratory habit. To test this theory, stork eggs were removed from their nest and hatched in the laboratory. After the adult wild storks had flown south, the baby storks were released from the laboratory. These young birds, who had never been in contact with other storks, immediately began their southward migration. They set off with great confidence, as if they had traveled the migratory route many times before.

factor that triggers migratory behavior. In an experiment, migratory birds were kept in artificially lighted rooms. It was found that if the periods of "daylight" were gradually shortened, and the periods of darkness lengthened proportionately, the glands of the birds became active. These glands secreted hormones which are chemicals that control numerous body functions. Shorter periods of daylight seem to change the birds' hormone balance, so that they retain more

Twice each year migratory birds travel
a route in the sky
How do migrating birds navigate? called a "flyway."
These north-south flyways follow the contours of the shoreline, river valleys, and mountain ranges.

45

In these flyways there are thousands of miles of trackless ocean with no landmarks to guide birds. How do they find their way? And how do newborn birds know where to fly?

There is much evidence that birds navigate by the sun and stars. On cloudy days migratory flocks fly in random directions; but if the sun or stars become visible, they resume a straight course. In one experiment an English shore bird, a Manx shearwater, was taken from its nest in Wales and sent across the Atlantic Ocean in a box. After being released in Boston, it flew three thousand miles back to its nesting ground in Wales in only twelve days. The shearwater could not possibly have found its way home by random exploration. It must have known instinctively the direction it had to fly in order to reach home. An albatross was transported four thousand miles from Midway Island in the Pacific to the Philippines. A month later, the bird had flown back to Midway.

One scientist placed some warblers in a glass cage within a planetarium (a spherical dome on which the images of the stars are projected). At migration time, these European birds all faced in the direction of North Africa, where they normally spend the winter. When the cages were turned, the birds moved so as to retain their position facing North Africa. When the projected stars were blanked out to simulate a cloudy night, the birds were confused, turning every which way. Apparently, these European warblers navigated by sighting on individual stars or constellations.

Species that migrate during the daylight hours seem to find their way by

Scientists band birds to trace their migratory routes. An aluminum band clamped loosely around the bird's leg urges the finder to contact the U. S. Fish and Wildlife Service.

sighting on the sun. Observations of penguins on a featureless ice cap proved that they moved steadily in one direction as long as the sun was visible. But on cloudy days they walked in a random direction. Experiments with penguins indicate that their built-in sense of time, or "biological clock," enables them to maintain a steady course, even as the sun changes position in the sky. Some birds may find their way with the help of both the sun and the stars. In theory, their built-in compass and biological clock should provide all the information needed to follow a precise course over the earth's surface.

Many migrating birds never reach their destination, but billions do complete a safe journey. Migratory birds seem to have great reserves of energy. They can fight winds and storms and fly at high altitudes for long periods. Scientists have used radar to track night-flying migratory birds and have followed them on foot through jungle and desert. But the mystery of bird migration has not yet been solved.

Activities for You

Knowing the migratory habits of the birds will enable

How can you invite birds to "visit"?

you to see many "strangers" as they pass through your neighborhood. Providing a place for these travelers to eat and drink is rewarded by the occasion to study them at close hand. Such a place is easy to construct. If it is cared for the year around, it will not only attract the migrant, but will become a visiting place for many local birds.

Feeding stations, bathing pans, drinking dishes and birdhouses can be purchased at a local feed or hardware store. On the other hand, building them can be fun.

Many discarded household objects can serve to make interesting and unique homes and food trays for birds.

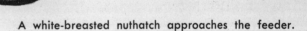

A white-breasted nuthatch approaches the feeder.

Mesh Cloth Feeder

A small board about eight inches square, to which a one-half-inch square mesh hardware cloth has been tacked, will hold suet. The birds feed by hanging to the wire and pecking through the mesh. This type of feeder can be nailed or screwed to a tree. Suet attracts the insect-eating birds.

Birdhouses

There are many good books in your public library on how to build birdhouses.

A. This is a good shape for a wren or bluebird house. If the bottom is made removable, it is easily cleaned.

B. Woodpeckers like a deep house and one this shape usually attracts them. It should be at least twelve inches high, with an opening of about two inches.

C. This feeder is easily constructed and can be made to your dimensions. It should be hung from a limb or pole to prevent mice or squirrels from reaching the food.